THE GREAT WEATHER INSIDE US:

A JOURNEY THROUGH EMOTIONS AND FEELINGS

BY

SELCURVE TEAM

This book belongs to:

____

Imprint: SELcurve
Paperback ISBN: 978-81-946896-9-0
Published By: Ustech Epublishers LLP

Website: www.SELcurve.com

A Letter to the Grown-ups

Welcome, dear nurturers of tomorrow's hearts and minds, to 'The Great Weather Inside Us.' Embarking on this journey is like opening a treasure chest of understanding, filled with the gems of emotional intelligence that are crucial for the growth of the children in your care. In this world, emotions are the weather patterns of the soul, ever-changing and rich with potential for learning and growth. Grasping the essence of our feelings is not just educational, but a profound step towards nurturing well-rounded, empathetic individuals. By acknowledging and understanding the full spectrum of our emotional climate, we empower our children to navigate the complexities of relationships and personal well-being with confidence and grace. This book is crafted to guide you through the intricate landscape of emotions and feelings, turning every page into a step towards emotional literacy and resilience.

How to Use This Book

Parents and teachers, you are the captains of this voyage, steering through the vast seas of emotions alongside your young explorers. Use this book as a compass to guide them through each chapter with care and attentiveness. It is designed to be a collaborative experience, encouraging discussions and reflections along the way. After each section, you will find interactive activities meant to deepen the connection between the concepts learned and the children's own inner worlds. It's not about rushing from chapter to chapter, but about taking the time to truly absorb and explore the emotions together. Let curiosity be your guide, and empathy your map, as you set off on this enlightening adventure through the heart's seasons with the young ones in your life.

Unlock Your Emotional Weather Adventure!

Ready for more fun and discovery? Scan this QR code to download your exclusive **FREE printable activities!** Each activity is a new adventure, helping you explore the wonderful world of emotions and feelings.

🌦️ **Discover and Play**: Find exciting games, thoughtful exercises, and creative challenges that bring the lessons of "The Great Weather Inside Us" to life!

🌈 **Learn and Grow**: These activities are perfect for sunny days, rainy afternoons, or anytime you want to dive deeper into understanding your own emotional weather.

🎈 **Share the Fun**: Bring friends and family into your journey of exploration. There's so much to learn and enjoy together!

So, grab your emotional weather gear and let's embark on this amazing adventure!

Contents

The Sky of Emotions

Exploring Emotions: Sailing Through the Sky of Feelings

Imagine gazing up so high,
At the vast and wondrous sky.
Sometimes it's sunny, bright and clear,
Other times clouds grey appear.

Just like the sky's ever-changing hue,
Inside us is something special too.
'Emotions' they are called, it's true,
The heart's way of chatting with me and you.

They tell us how we're **feeling** deep,
A **language** that our hearts do keep.
All around the world, in every **nation**,
People feel this inner **sensation**.

Emotions are like our **weather** inside,
Changing like **tides**, in which we confide.
They **rise** and **fall**, like waves at **sea**,
Part of us all, **uniquely** free.

Sunny **emotions**, bright and gay,
When **joy** and **laughter** come our way.
Like sunshine **rays** that warmly **hug**,
In our **hearts**, they're snug as a bug.

Then come the **clouds**, gray and wide,
When **sadness** makes our hearts reside,
Heavy like **rain**, soft and slow,
In these moments, our **feelings** flow.

Stormy **anger**, loud and **fierce**,
Like **thunder** in our chests, it pierces.
Rumbling, tumbling, strong and **stark**,
Lightning flashes in the dark.

But **calm** emotions too, take part,
Peaceful, still, they soothe the **heart**.
Like a **lake**, so smooth and **clear**,
In these moments, **serenity** is near.

Recognizing Emotions: Spotting Clouds and Sunbeams

Now, how do we know what emotion we're feeling? It's like being a weather detective! Here are some fun ways to discover the weather inside:

Emotion Mirror Game:

Stand in front of a mirror with a friend or family member. Take turns making faces that show different emotions like happiness, surprise, or confusion. Guess each other's emotion-weather and see who can get it right!

Emotion Story Time:

Think of a time when you felt a strong emotion. Draw a picture of that moment and share it with someone, explaining why you felt that way. Was it sunny, rainy, or maybe a little foggy in your heart?

Weather Report Role Play:

Pretend you're a weather reporter, but instead of talking about the weather outside, report on how you're feeling inside. "Today, there's a bit of surprise with a chance of excitement!"

By playing these games, you'll become an expert at knowing all the different kinds of weather inside you, and soon, you'll be able to understand not just your own emotions, but your friends' and family's emotional weather too!

The Landscape of Feelings

Emotions to Feelings: Journey Across the Heart's Terrain

Now we know, in our hearts so smart,
Emotions are like weather's art.
And feelings, oh, they're stories bright,
The tales that weather whispers light.

If emotions are the sky's own play,
Feelings are the tales they say.
Like a sunny day brings picnic cheer,
Or soccer games we hold so dear.

The same sun can warm different tales,
As the heart's weather sails and scales.
Each moment, each place, each friendly face,
Gives feelings a unique embrace.

Take **excitement**, lively and bright,
It can **transform**, much to our delight.
When you **win** a race, proud feelings soar,
Like an **eagle's** flight, it's something more.

Or when a new **adventure** book you begin,
Curiosity bubbles up within.
The emotion's the same, a **sparkling** flame,
But the feeling shifts with the game's **name**.

Each **experience**, like a different key,
Plays a tune on emotion's **sea**.
The emotion stays, but feelings **sway**,
Dancing differently every day.

Feeling Stories: Narratives from the Emotional Landscape

Let's imagine some stories to see how the same emotion leads to different feelings:

The Birthday Surprise:

Jamie felt a rush of surprise when her friends jumped out and yelled "Surprise!" at her birthday party. That surprise turned into joy and happiness as she realized they were all there to celebrate with her.

The Hidden Path:

Alex felt the same surprise as Jamie when he discovered a hidden path in the woods. But for him, that surprise turned into wonder and amazement as he explored a place he had never seen before.

The Lost Toy:

Sam felt a pang of sadness when he couldn't find his favorite toy. That sadness turned into loneliness because he felt like no one understood how important it was to him.

The New Friend:

Lily felt the same sadness when she had to say goodbye to her friend who was moving away. But for her, that sadness turned into hope when she made a new friend who shared her love for painting.

Emotions like surprise and sadness can lead to many different feelings based on our stories. In the next chapters, we'll explore more about each emotion and the beautiful landscape of feelings they can create.

Remember:

Every feeling tells a story, and your story is as unique as you are!

Sunny Days - Feeling Happy

Basking in Happiness: Soaking Up the Joyful Sun

Have you felt like a **balloon**, so light,
Floating up in the sky, **sunny** and bright?
That's **happiness**, bubbly and right,
Light as **air**, a delightful sight!

When your inner sun **shines**, oh so grand,
Spreading **joy** across the land.
It's like **smiling** just because you can,
Happiness, a cheerful, glowing fan.

You can spot **happiness**, here's how it shows,
Maybe your **feet** dance, from tips to your toes.
Your voice may sing like a **bird** in spring,
Even saying, 'Pass the carrots,' makes your **heart** zing!

When happy, you might want to **share** your toys,
Spread the **joy** to all the girls and boys.
Or give a **hug**, big and snug,
To **friends** and family, a love-filled tug.

Sharing Happiness: Spreading Sunshine

Now, what can you do with this sunny feeling? Let's share it, like clouds share rain to help flowers grow! Here are some fun sunshine activities:

The Happiness Circle:

Sit in a circle with your friends or family. One person starts by saying something that makes them happy, then tosses a yellow ball (like a little sun) to someone else. Keep tossing the ball around and listen to all the happy things—it's like collecting rays of sunshine!

The Smile Challenge:

How many people can you make smile today? Give it a try! You can smile, tell a funny joke, or just say something kind. Keep track with happy face stickers on a chart.

Happy Notes:

Draw a sunny picture or write a happy note and give it to someone. It could be your teacher, a friend, or even the mail carrier. Spreading happiness can be that simple and fun!

Remember:

When you share your happiness, it's like planting little seeds of joy that can grow into a garden of smiles all around you. Let's be happiness gardeners together!

Rainy Moods - Feeling Sad

Embracing Sadness: Understanding the Rainy Days

Sometimes our inner sky turns gray,
Under a cloud, we might stay.
This is sadness, soft and low,
It's okay to let this feeling show.

Everyone feels a bit blue,
Just like rainy days come too.
Sadness might be wanting space,
Or tears gently rolling down your face.

Maybe it's quiet, a hush so deep,
Like the world's gone still, in a sleepy heap.
It's a part of us, like night to day,
Sadness, in its own way, has a say.

But guess what? Sadness, like rain, has its place,
A message from the heart, in its own pace.
It says, 'Hey, something's off, let's take it slow,
To think, to understand, to gently grow.'

When sadness visits, give yourself a hug,
With calming things that feel snug as a bug.
Draw a picture, let your colors flow,
Listen to music soft and low.

Or cuddle your stuffed animal tight,
In its fluffy warmth, find delight.
Sadness, like a cloud, will drift away,
Making room for another day.

The Upside of Rain: Finding Beauty in the Raindrops

You know, **rain's** not just a wet affair,
It helps the **flowers** bloom with care.
Rivers flow, thanks to its touch,
Rain does so much, oh **so much**.

Just like rain, **sadness** has a role,
In your **growth**, it plays a part whole.
When you're sad, you start to **see**,
Your feelings, what **matters**, what the needs be.

You learn about what **stirs** inside,
What's **important**, what can't hide.
And how to make things feel **alright**,
In sadness' soft, reflective **light**.

And here's a **secret**, lean in close,
When you know your **rain**, the sun **boasts**.
Understanding rainy **moods**, you see,
Makes **sunny** days brighter, filled with glee.

You learn to **cherish** happy times more,
And when others are sad, you **don't** ignore.
Being **kind** to them, showing you care,
In their rainy days, you're there to **share**.

Rainy Day Activities: Your Umbrella in the Rain

Now, what can you do when there are clouds of sadness in your heart? Let's explore some activities that are like umbrellas and raincoats for our hearts, helping us to embrace and move through sadness in our own cozy way:

Feeling Raindrops:

When you're sad, find a window and watch the rain. Each raindrop can be a feeling. Imagine those feelings dripping down outside, washing away, and making room for a new day.

The Cozy Fort:

Build a fort with pillows and blankets. Inside your cozy space, you can think, rest, or read a comforting story. It's like making a safe place for your feelings until the sun comes back.

Color the Clouds:

Draw or paint how you feel when you're sad. Use colors like blue or gray. This is a way to let out sadness without having to use words.

Remember:

Everyone has rainy days, but the sun always comes back. And just like after the rain, everything can feel fresh and new again. So, let's put on our rain boots, jump in some puddles, and know that sunny smiles are just around the corner!

Thunder and Lightning – Feeling Angry

Inside Anger: The Storm Brewing Within

Just like a **thunderstorm**, quick and loud,
Anger can boom in us, a stormy cloud.
Suddenly, it crackles, bursts, and **roars**,
Inside us, like **thunder's** mighty snores.

When angry, you might feel a fiery **heat**,
Your heart racing fast, **skipping** a beat.
Wanting to **stomp**, like thunder's drum,
Rumbling feet, here they come.

Anger is strong, a powerful wave,
Feeling it's normal, no need to be brave.
It's your mind's shout, a loud 'Hey there!',
Saying, 'Something's wrong, please be aware!'

Maybe a toy was taken, not a word said,
Or plans got changed, filling you with dread.
It's alright to feel this stormy way,
But what you do next holds the key to the day.

With thunder and lightning stirring inside,
Choosing your actions is where wisdom resides.
It's in how you handle this stormy spell,
That shows your heart's story, the tale it will tell.

Calming the Storm: Taming the Thunder and Lightning

When anger strikes, it's time to be like a weather forecaster and predict the storm before it gets too wild. Here are some ways to calm the thunder and keep your lightning safe:

Deep Breaths:

Take deep breaths in and out, like you're blowing up a giant balloon. This helps cool down your mind and makes the angry storm clouds start to disappear.

Count to Ten:

When you're feeling angry, count slowly to ten. By the time you reach ten, you might find that the storm isn't as strong and you can think more clearly.

Storm in a Bottle:

Fill a bottle with water, glitter, and glue.
When you shake it, it looks like a storm!
Watch the glitter settle to the bottom, and
as it does, let your anger settle too.

Anger Scribbles:

Grab some paper and a crayon, and
scribble as hard as you want. Let the paper
feel the storm, not the people around you.

Remember:

Just like thunder and lightning, anger can be loud and scary, but it
always passes. And after, you can see things clearer, just like the air feels
fresher after a storm. So next time you feel a storm brewing inside, you
know how to calm it down and make it okay again.

The Fog of Fear

Navigating Fear: A Walk Through the Misty Fog

Have you stood in a **fog**, thick and gray,
Where what's ahead is **hidden** away?
That's **fear**, wrapping around like a mist,
Making the clear and known seem to **twist**.

When scared, our **hearts** pound like a drum,
Beating fast, oh, here it comes.
Palms may sweat, a river's **flow**,
And our feet **itch** to run, to go.

Fear cloaks us in a shroud of doubt,
Turning **certainty** inside out.
It's a feeling, deep and **profound**,
In its **mist**, we sometimes are found.

Fear is sneaky, it can jump out,
When new things come about, no doubt.
It's like an alarm, ringing loud and clear,
Telling us to watch out, be aware, my dear.

It helps us stay safe, to mind our way,
In caution's embrace, we safely stay.
Like fearing a stove, so hot and fierce,
It warns us, 'Don't touch! Let safety persevere.'

Fear's a guardian in its own right,
Helping us navigate the unknowns in sight.
In new adventures or places unseen,
Fear keeps us alert, our judgment keen.

Brave Explorers: Finding Courage in the Haze

Even when fear feels as thick as fog, we can be brave explorers. Here are some activities that can help you become a master of the mist and find your way through the fog of fear:

The Map of Bravery:

Draw a map of a place you feel safe, like your bedroom or a park. When you're scared, imagine yourself in this place and remember the calm and safe feeling.

Fear Binoculars:

Make binoculars out of paper rolls. Look through them when you're scared, and pretend you can see right through the fog to the fun or calm on the other side.

Monster Spray: Create a special spray with water and a few drops of a nice-smelling oil. Whenever you're scared, especially at night, spray it around to keep the 'monsters' away.

Bravery Badge: Make a badge with paper and colors that you can wear whenever you need a little extra courage. It's your secret armor against fear.

Remember:

Being brave doesn't mean you aren't scared. It means you face the foggy fear and walk through it anyway. Each step you take is like a ray of sunshine cutting through the fog, and soon, you'll see the clear path ahead. You're much braver than you think!

The Rainbow of Surprises

The Colors of Surprise: Painting the Unexpected

Imagine a walk, post-rainy day's cheer,
Suddenly, a rainbow, vividly clear.
What a surprise, across the sky,
Like a gift unseen, catching the eye.

Or when a friend jumps out with a 'Boo!',
Surprise jumps in, saying 'How do you do?'
It's the feeling when unexpected things pop,
Making our eyes widen, jaws might drop.

When something **happens**, out of the blue,
Surprise says 'Hello! I'm here for you!'
Eyes go round, mouths open **wide**,
In the world of **surprise**, we take a ride.

Sometimes **surprises** bring joy and **delight**,
Like hearing you're off to the **park**, what a sight!
Other times, they startle, give a little **fright**,
Like a **loud** noise bursting in the night.

Surprises can make our hearts skip and leap,
Then dance to a **beat** that's fast and deep.
In their unexpected **twist** and turn,
Excitement and wonder in us burn.

Unpredictable Weather: Embracing Life's Surprises

Just like weather, life can be full of surprises. One day it's sunny, and the next day it might rain. But just as we carry an umbrella for unexpected rain, we can learn to adapt to life's surprises:

The Surprise Box:

Create a 'Surprise Box' with different items inside. Pick one out each day, and think about how it could be a surprise. Is it something that makes you laugh, or maybe something that teaches you?

Weather Reporter Game:

Pretend to be a weather reporter, but with a twist! Report sunny weather and then suddenly switch to rain or snow. It's a fun way to learn that surprises can change things quickly, and we can still smile and go with the flow.

Surprise Story Time:

Make up stories with surprising endings. This can show you that even when things don't go as planned, they can still turn out to be great adventures.

Remember:

Just like a rainbow after the rain, surprises can bring color and excitement to our lives. When something surprising happens, take a deep breath and look for the rainbow. It might be the start of an amazing new adventure!

The Warmth of Love

Feeling the Warmth: Embracing the Embrace

Close your eyes, take a moment, and **see**,
A **loving** hug, as warm as can be.
Or **snuggling** with your pet, so dear,
Or a **best friend's** smile, bringing cheer.

That's **love!** A warmth, a special glow,
Filling our hearts, making **feelings** flow.
It's like **sunshine**, cozy and bright,
Nurturing our garden with **gentle** light.

In this sunshine, feelings **bloom**,
In love's **embrace**, they find room.
A garden of **emotions**, rich and grand,
Grows in the heart, **hand in hand**.

Love is about sharing, far and wide,
Your favorite toy, or a slide down the slide.
A helping hand to a friend who's down,
Or sweet words that wipe away a frown.

It's a special joy, a unique light,
That makes not just you feel bright.
But spreads a glow, a kind delight,
To those around, in day and night.

This love, a gift we freely give,
In every moment that we live.
It's happiness that we share,
Showing others how much we care.

Just like plants need care to grow, love flourishes with every kind act and tender word. Here are some lovely ways to help your love grow:

Kindness Cards:

Draw or write cards for people you care about. Tell them what makes them special. It's like planting a seed of happiness in their heart.

Helping Hands:

Doing little helpful things, like setting the table or watering plants, shows love without needing any words at all. It's like the silent sunshine that helps your family's love grow.

Gratitude Moments:

Share what you're thankful for about each person in your family. Maybe it's mom's cooking or dad's funny stories. Gratitude is like the rain that helps love grow strong and deep.

Remember:

Every kind action is like a bloom in the garden of love. The more you nurture it, the more love will blossom around you. So let's put on our gardening gloves and spread love in every way, every day!

The Whirlwind of Frustration

Taming the Whirlwind: Understanding Frustration's Twist

Frustration's a **whirlwind**, swirling inside,
Tossing thoughts and feelings on a **bumpy ride**.
When it strikes, fists might clench **tight**,
Brows **furrowed**, in the dimming light.

A storm of **sighs**, a rush, a race,
Like puzzles with pieces out of **place**.
Or reaching for **cookies**, just too high,
Frustration makes us **heave** a sigh.

It twirls around, like **leaves** in the wind,
Searching for calm, **peace** to find.

A challenge, yes, but one we meet,
As we stand tall, not accepting defeat.

Frustration crops up, now and then,
When plans go awry, again and again.
Maybe a math problem, tough as can be,
Or a tower of blocks that just won't agree.

It falls and tumbles, down to the ground,
That twisty, tangled feeling is found.
When things feel too hard, and won't fit right,
Frustration lurks, just out of sight.

It's the knot inside when things won't bend,
To our will, our wish, right to the end.
A puzzle of sorts, with pieces astray,
That's frustration's twisty, tangled way.

Calming the Twister: Strategies to Settle the Swirl

When the whirlwind of frustration starts to spin, it's time to become the calm in the center of the storm. Here are some ways to smooth out the winds of frustration and find your peace:

The Frustration Flip:

Take a deep breath and try to flip your thinking. Instead of focusing on what's making you frustrated, think of one thing you've done well today. It's like turning the wind of frustration into a gentle breeze.

Stretch Out the Frustration:

When you feel wound up, try stretching your arms and legs. Imagine letting the frustration flow out through your fingertips and toes, releasing it into the air like a kite in the wind.

Frustration Doodles:

Grab some paper and doodle out your frustration. You can draw squiggles, zigzags, or whatever feels right. Watching your feelings take shape on paper can help calm the whirlwind inside.

Talk About the Twister:

Share your feelings with someone you trust. Sometimes, just talking about what's frustrating you can help settle the swirling storm. It's like having a friend help you find the eye of the whirlwind, where everything is calm.

Remember:

Frustration is like a gusty wind – it can whip around and be unsettling, but eventually, it settles down. With these tools, you can tame the whirlwind of frustration and find your calm, sunny day again.

The Mist of Disappointment

Peering Through Disappointment: A Glimpse Beyond the Mist

Disappointment's like a **balloon**, losing air,
Deflating slowly, in its quiet **despair**.
Shoulders **droop** down, like branches heavy,
A smile turns to **frown**, in life's unsteady levy.

It's that sinking **feeling**, deep and low,
When things don't turn out, as **hoped** in the flow.
Like waiting for **sun**, but getting rain,
A twist in the **tale**, a silent refrain.

When **excitement** meets a different fate,
Not as grand as **imagined**, a change in state.
Disappointment whispers, soft and plain,
Like a quiet melody, a softer **strain**.

Disappointment is natural, it's true,
Like a cloudy sky, a different view.
It happens when hopes don't quite align,
Like a canceled playdate, or a lost sunshine.

Or not getting the part you wished to play,
In the school drama, in its array.
Feeling this way is normal, part of the quest,
But it's how we navigate that's the true test.

Through the cloudy mist, we find a path,
A way to smile, to laugh, to craft.
It's in these moments, we find our light,
Guiding us through, making everything right.

Clearing the Fog: Pathways Out of Disappointment

When disappointment drifts in, it's like navigating through a fog. Here are some ways to find your path through the mist and back into the sunshine:

Gratitude List:

Start by thinking of three things you are grateful for. It's like finding patches of blue sky on a cloudy day. This can help lift the mist of disappointment and remind you of the good things you still have.

Disappointment Diary:

Grab a notebook and write or draw about your disappointment. Pouring your feelings onto paper can make them feel lighter, like letting go of a balloon and watching it float away.

Talk It Out:

Share your feelings with someone you trust. Just talking about what disappointed you can make the fog feel less thick. It's like having a friend help guide you through the mist with a bright lantern.

Find the Silver Lining:

Look for something positive in the situation. Maybe you didn't get the role you wanted, but you can try a different and exciting part. Finding the silver lining is like a ray of sunshine peeking through the clouds.

Remember:

Just like the weather, our feelings change too. Disappointment is like a misty morning that clears up as the day goes on. With these strategies, you'll find your way through the fog and back into the bright, sunny day.

The Breezy Day of Excitement

Feeling Excitement: Like a Sunny, Windy Day

Excitement's like a day so sunny,
With a breeze that's playful, sweet as honey.
It tickles like the wind, full of glee,
Making eyes twinkle, as happy as can be.

Words zoom out fast, like leaves in a dance,
On the wind's lively tune, in its merry prance.
This feeling's as fun as leaves in a whirl,
Swirling in colors, in a joyful twirl.

It's a burst of happy, bright and clear,
Like a windy day, full of cheer.
Excitement's a buzz, an energetic spree,
A whirlwind of joy, wild and free.

Think of the times, full of **wonder** and cheer,
Like a birthday **party**, soon to be here.
Or a trip to the **zoo**, a new adventure's call,
Or opening a **book**, in autumn or fall.

Excitement's that bubbly, **giggly** feel,
In your tummy, spinning like a **wheel**.
Just like running **free** on a breezy day,
Happy and **light**, in every way.

It's the joy of waiting for something **grand**,
Like footprints in the **sand**, hand in hand.
Excitement's a dance, a playful **spree**,
A heart full of **laughter**, light and free.

Balancing Excitement: Keeping Your Kite in the Sky

Excitement is great, but sometimes it's like a kite flying too high and fast. Here are some fun ways to enjoy excitement while keeping your feet on the ground:

The Excitement Dance:

When you're full of excitement, do a happy dance! Move your body to the beat of your heart, like leaves swirling in the wind. This dance lets you have fun with your excitement and share it with the world.

Excitement Countdown:

If you're excited about something coming soon, make a countdown calendar. Each day you cross off brings you closer to the fun, just like counting the days to the next sunny, windy day.

Quiet Time:

Take a break and sit quietly for a little while. Breathe in and out, and imagine your excitement like a soft breeze inside you. This helps your excitement feel just right, not too wild.

Excitement Share:

Talk about what makes you excited with a friend or family. Sharing your excitement can make it even better, like sharing the fun of playing outside on a windy day.

Remember:

Excitement is like a bright, windy day – full of energy and smiles. But it's also important to enjoy it in a way that's fun and safe. With these activities, you can ride the breezy waves of excitement while staying happy and calm, just like a perfect day outside.

The Cloudy Day of Disgust

Understanding Disgust: Like a Whiff of Stinky Air

Disgust is like **scrunching** your nose tight,
When something smells **bad**, not quite right.
Or turning away from a **yucky** sight,
It's that **'Ew!'** feeling, in day or night.

When you **see**, smell, or taste something off,
Like spoiled food, or a **cough**.
Or a muddy **puddle**, messy and deep,
Disgust makes a jump, a big, bold **leap**.

It's a face of 'no thanks', a clear **'no way'**,
When things aren't **pleasant**, in your day.
Disgust is clear, in its own way,
Telling us what to keep at **bay**.

Think of **disgust** as a hero in disguise,
Alerting you when something's **unwise**.
Like a superhero saying, 'Beware of that **puddle!'**
Saving your shoes from a muddy **muddle**.

It's your body's way of saying, 'This might not be **great,'**
A **cautionary** signal, before it's too late.
Feeling **'Ew!'** is okay, it's part of the plan,
To keep you from **harm**, as best as it can.

It's good to know **why**, to understand the cause,
Why some things give us a moment's **pause**.
Disgust has a role, in its own special way,
Helping us decide what's okay and what's **nay**.

Responding to Disgust: Solving the Stinky Puzzle

Disgust can feel like a puzzle, but you can learn to understand it without feeling too yucky. Let's try some fun ways to figure it out:

Disgust Detective:

Pretend you're a detective and find out what makes you feel "Ew." Is it the smell of old socks or the sight of slimy snails? Draw or write about it. Knowing more about your disgust can help you handle that "Ew!" feeling.

Disgust Discussion:

Chat with a friend, parent, or teacher about what grosses you out. Talking about it can make it feel less yucky, and you might learn that others feel the same way or even differently.

Exploring Solutions:

If something specific makes you feel "Ew," think of ways to fix it. For example, if a messy room gives you the yuckies, cleaning up a bit might make things better. Solving the yucky problem can make you feel more in charge.

Disgust and Curiosity:

Be a little curious about the yucky things. Ask yourself, "Why does this gross me out?" Maybe it's not always so bad, and sometimes it's okay. Being curious can make disgust a bit more interesting.

Remember:

Disgust is just one part of how we feel, like a cloudy day in the world of our emotions. When we understand our disgust and know how to respond to it, it's like solving a puzzle. And when the puzzle is complete, everything starts to make more sense, even the yucky parts!

When Emotions Mix - Confusing Clouds

Mixed Emotions: Navigating the Foggy Intersection

Have you felt like a smoothie, blended and bright,
With different fruits, each a bite of delight?
Mixed together, they create a new taste,
Just like our emotions, in their own haste.

Sometimes happy from playing with friends,
Yet a bit sad when the day ends.
Or excited for a trip, a new place to roam,
But nervous about the journey from home.

This is called mixed emotions, a colorful blend,
Where different feelings mix and bend.
It's perfectly normal, part of the day,
Like a smoothie of emotions, in their own way.

Think of your **heart** as the sky so wide,
Where **weather** dances and likes to hide.
Most days, it's one kind, clear and **true**,
Sunny or rainy, with a simple view.

But sometimes, the sky gets **creative** and bright,
Mixing the weather, a **delightful** sight.
A **rainbow** there, or a sun-shower here,
Nature's art, crystal clear.

Our **emotions** are like this, you see,
Mixing together, **wild** and free.
Combining to form **feelings** new,
A tapestry of **emotions**, with every hue.

The Colorful Clouds Game: Painting the Emotional Sky

Let's play a game to see how our mixed emotions can make new shades, just like colors do!

You'll need:

- Paint or colored pencils in basic colors (red, blue, yellow, white, black)
- Paper
- A heart full of imagination!

Instructions:

- Think of a color for each emotion: red for anger, blue for sadness, yellow for happiness, black for fear, and white for calm.
- On your paper, mix two colors to see what new color you get. Red and blue make purple, right?
- Now, mix the emotions like you mixed the colors. If you felt happy (yellow) and a little scared (black), you might feel excited (green).
- Talk about this new feeling with someone. What does it feel like? When have you felt it before?

Remember:

Just like in our game, our emotions can mix and make us feel things we didn't expect, and that's okay! It's all part of the great big world of feelings inside us.

Understanding Others - Empathy Breezes

Feeling Together: The Winds of Empathy

Imagine a **superpower**, special and true,
Feeling what **others** feel, just by their view.
A warm wind, **empathy**, it's called by name,
Helping you feel what others frame.

Empathy is sharing, understanding too,
What **friends** and family are going through.
Like seeing a friend who's had a **fall**,
You feel their **pain**, answer empathy's call.

It's knowing it hurts, feeling their **sorrow**,
Wishing them a brighter **tomorrow**.
Empathy's a gift, from heart to heart,
A magical bond, an emotional **art**.

Empathy's a breeze, gentle and soft,
Connecting us all, aloft.
It whispers secrets, feelings, and more,
Showing us what others have in store.

When we listen to this quiet wind,
Understanding others, we find.
We become a friend, good and true,
A caring sibling, through and through.

Or a helpful classmate, kind and wise,
Seeing the world through others' eyes.
Empathy's the bridge, the link that binds,
In every heart, it gently winds.

Walking in Their Shoes: A Journey of Understanding

Let's practice using our superpower of empathy with a fun activity!

You'll need:

- A few simple costumes or props (like hats, glasses, or anything you think could help you pretend to be someone else)
- A list of scenarios (like someone being sad because they lost their favorite toy or being happy because they learned to ride a bike)

Instructions:

- Pick a scenario and a costume or prop.
- Pretend you are the person in the scenario. How do you think they feel? Why do they feel that way?
- Share those feelings with a friend or family member. Can they guess what happened just by how you're acting?
- Now, switch! Let them wear the costume and you guess the feeling.

By pretending to be someone else, we can get a little taste of their feelings. This game helps us practice empathy, so when it's time to be a real superhero friend, we're ready with our superpower of understanding!

Navigating Hard Feelings - The Compass of Control

Steering Through Tough Feelings: Jealousy and Envy

Sometimes feelings, deep and vast,
Make us feel like we're lost, aghast.
Like at sea, in waves so high,
With tough emotions, we might sigh.

Imagine jealousy, a green wave tall,
Rising up when we see someone's haul.
Something they have, we wish was ours,
A feeling that overpowers.

Envy's close, a whispering breeze,
Telling us 'I want that, please'.
Wishing to be like someone who,
Has what's cool, or better, true.

It's a longing, a silent cry,
For things others have, making us sigh.
These feelings, like sea and wind,
Show desires that are pinned.

These feelings are normal, part of our map,
But like a ship with a compass, we can adapt.
Steering through choppy waters, emotions run deep,
We learn to navigate, not just to weep.

Remember, it's okay to feel this spin,
But acting mean, let's not begin.
Our feelings, though strong, should not lead,
To hurting others, in word or deed.

Like sailors, wise, on the ocean's sway,
We choose how to act, how to display.
With kindness and care, our course we chart,
Guided by the compass of the heart.

Finding Direction: Charting a Course Through Emotional Seas

Now, let's find our compass and map to help guide us through:

You'll need:

- Drawing materials (like paper, crayons, or markers)
- An 'Emotion Compass' drawn on a piece of paper with different emotions pointing in different directions

Instructions:

- When you feel a tough emotion like jealousy or envy, take out your 'Emotion Compass'.
- Draw or write about what made you feel that way. Is it because a friend has a new toy? Or maybe someone won a prize?
- Now, think about what you have that makes you special. Maybe you're really good at drawing or you have a big, loving family.
- Draw these good things around your 'Emotion Compass'. This is your treasure map of happiness!
- Every time you feel lost in tough feelings, look at your map and remember the treasures you have in your life.

This activity helps us learn that even when tough feelings try to steer us off course, we have a compass of control to help us find the right direction. It shows us that every feeling has its place, and we can learn from all of them to become better treasure hunters in the journey of our emotions.

Weather Report - Checking In With Yourself

Daily Emotion Forecast: Understanding Your Internal Weather

Just like the weather, ever so fleet,
From sunny to rainy, or windy beat,
Our feelings change, shift, and sway,
A different 'emotional weather' each day.

Are you sunny and bright, a clear sky's hue,
Or is there a storm inside of you?
Checking in with feelings, each and all,
Is like being a forecaster, having a ball.

Being your own weather guide, so keen,
Understanding emotions, seen and unseen.
Are they calm or in a whirl,
In your inner world, emotions unfurl.

Every **morning**, as the day begins,
Ask **yourself**, amid the life's spins,
'How am I **feeling**, on this day?'
Happy, sad, excited, in **which** way?

You might be a **mix**, a blend so vast,
Of **feelings** from the future and past.
Talking about them, clear and **loud**,
Is like sharing the **weather**, making you proud.

It's like a daily **weather report**,
Telling others of your emotional **sort**.
This helps them know, in sun or **rain**,
How to **support** you, in joy or pain.

The Emotional Weather Station: Building Your Inner Barometer

Let's make your very own Emotional Weather Station!

You will need:

- Construction paper or cardboard
- Markers or paint
- Split pins (brads)
- Templates of different weather symbols (like a sun, clouds, rain, snow, and a rainbow)
- A big arrow to point to your 'emotional weather'

Instructions:

- Cut out a large circle from your cardboard or construction paper. This is your main weather board.
- Decorate your weather board with the markers or paint. You can write "My Emotional Weather Station" at the top.
- Cut out the weather symbols and place them around the board. Each symbol represents a feeling (happy, sad, angry, scared, excited, etc.).
- In the center of the board, attach the big arrow with a split pin so it can spin around.
- Each day, spin the arrow to the 'weather' that matches how you're feeling.
- If it points to the sunny symbol, you're feeling happy. If it points to the rain, maybe you're feeling a bit sad. It's okay to have any kind of weather because it helps us understand and care for our feelings better. Plus, when you know your weather, you can dress for it – with a smile, a hug, or maybe a quiet space to think.

By checking in with your Emotional Weather Station every day, you learn to understand and express your feelings. It's a great way to start the day, ready for whatever weather comes your way!

The Emotional Weather Map: Navigating Our Feelings

Happiness (Sunny Day): "Like a sunny day, happiness fills our hearts with warmth and light."

Fear (Foggy Mist): "Fear is a foggy mist that can make things seem unclear or scary."

Sadness (Rainy Day): "Sadness is like gentle rain, sometimes needed, bringing quiet moments of reflection."

Surprise (Rainbow): "Surprise is a colorful rainbow, suddenly brightening our world in unexpected ways."

Anger (Thunderstorm): "Anger can be fierce like a thunderstorm, rumbling with energy and noise."

Love (Warm Breeze): "Love is a warm breeze, softly touching our lives with care and kindness."

Jealousy (Wilted Plant): "Jealousy is like a wilted plant under a cloud, longing for what others have."

Excitement (Breezy Day): "Excitement is a breezy day, full of energy and fluttering leaves of anticipation."

Envy (Green Rain): "Envy feels like green rain, wanting what falls in others' gardens."

Disgust (Stinky Smell): "Disgust is a stinky smell that scrunches our noses and makes us turn away.

Frustration (Whirlwind): "Frustration swirls like a whirlwind, tossing our thoughts and feelings around."

Mixed Emotions (Partly Cloudy): "Mixed emotions are like a partly cloudy sky, where sun and rain mix together.""

Disappointment (Overcast Sky): "Disappointment is a gray sky, clouding over our sunny expectations."

Empathy (Gentle Rain): "Empathy is like gentle rain that nurtures and understands the flowers of our feelings."

The Journey Continues

Hey there, amazing explorers, so bright!
You've learned about emotions, day and night.
From sunny smiles that light up the day,
To stormy frowns, and surprises that play.

But guess what? This is just the start,
Of a journey fantastic, a work of heart.
Your feelings, like a sky so wide,
Changing and growing, side by side.

Each day, a new chance to explore,
Your feelings, a vast, unopened door.
Are they wild like wind, or calm as night?
Remember, they're okay, and you're just right.

Keep sharing how you **feel**, talk and say,
And listen to **friends**, as they convey.
Their **weather reports**, their stories too,
Helping each other, that's what we **do**.

On this special **journey**, we all partake,
Learning and growing, for each other's **sake**.
So, keep exploring, under the sky so **vast**,
In the world of **emotions**, you'll have a blast.

A Note for Parents and Teachers

Dear adults who care so much,

You've been the wind helping our little ones soar on this emotional weather adventure. Thank you for guiding them through the cloudy and sunny days alike.

We want to keep supporting you, too! On our SEL Curve platform, you'll find more resources, like articles and activities, to continue this important work. Our tips and tools are designed to make learning about emotions fun and meaningful.

Remember to check in with your own emotional weather, because taking care of yourself helps you be there for the children.

Together, we're building a world where every child can understand their emotions and grow up feeling confident, caring, and ready for all kinds of weather. Keep the conversation going, and watch them flourish!

With heartfelt thanks,

Your SEL Curve Team

www.selcurve.com

Appendix

A Summary of All Chapters

Chapter 1: The Sky of Emotions

Imagine looking up at the sky. Sometimes it's bright and sunny, other times it's cloudy and grey. Just like the sky, we have something special inside us called 'emotions.' Emotions are the way our heart talks to us about how we are feeling, and everyone around the world has them. They're like our inner weather!

There are sunny emotions, like when we feel joy and laughter bubbles up inside us like rays of sunshine. Then there are the cloudy ones, like sadness, when our heart feels a bit heavy, as if it's going to rain. We also have stormy emotions, like anger, where we might feel like thunder is rumbling in our chests. And there are also calm emotions, like when we feel peaceful and our heart is as still as a smooth lake.

Chapter 2: The Landscape of Feelings

Now that we know emotions are like the weather in our hearts, let's talk about feelings. If emotions are the weather, feelings are the stories that weather tells. Just like how a sunny day can make a picnic fun or a game of soccer exciting, the same emotion can make us feel different things based on what is happening around us.

For example, the emotion of excitement can turn into the feeling of being proud when you win a race, or it can become the feeling of curiosity when you start a new adventure book. The emotion is the same, but the feeling changes with the experience.

Chapter 3: Sunny Days – Feeling Happy

Have you ever felt like you're a balloon, floating up into the sky on a sunny day? That's what happiness can feel like—light, bubbly, and bright! Happiness is when your inner sun is shining so much that you might even feel like smiling for no reason at all.

You can recognize happiness in many ways. Maybe your feet start to do a little dance. Perhaps your voice sounds like a cheerful song, even when you're just saying, "Pass the carrots, please!" When you're happy, you might feel like sharing your toys more or giving a big, warm hug to your friends and family.

Chapter 4: Rainy Moods – Feeling Sad

Sometimes, our inner sky gets cloudy, and it feels like we're under a gray blanket. This is sadness, and it's okay to feel this way. Everyone feels sad sometimes—just like everyone has rainy days. Sadness can feel like wanting to be alone, having a little cry, or just being quiet.

But guess what? Just like rain, your sadness is there for a reason. It's your heart's way of saying, "Hey, something is not right, and I need to slow down and think about it." So, when you're sad, give yourself a hug by doing things that are calming, like drawing, listening to soft music, or cuddling your favorite stuffed animal.

The Upside of Rain:

You know, rain isn't just about getting wet. It helps flowers to grow and rivers to flow. And just like that, your sadness can help you grow too. When you're sad, you learn about your feelings, what matters to you, and what you need to feel better.

And here's a secret: when you understand your rainy moods, the sunny days become even brighter! You learn to enjoy your happy moments more and to be kind to others when they feel sad.

Chapter 5: Thunder and Lightning – Feeling Angry

Just like a sudden thunderstorm, anger can boom and crackle inside us without warning. When you're angry, you might feel hot, your heart might beat faster, and you might want to stomp your feet like thunder rumbling.

Anger is a strong emotion, and it's perfectly normal to feel it. It's like your mind's way of saying, "Hey, something is not okay!" Maybe a friend took your toy without asking, or you couldn't do something you really wanted to do. It's okay to feel this way, but what's important is what you do with the thunder and lightning inside.

Chapter 6: The Fog of Fear

Have you ever been surrounded by a thick fog when you can't see what's ahead? That's how fear can feel sometimes. It wraps around us and makes everything feel unsure. When we're scared, our hearts might beat like a drum, our palms might get sweaty, and we might feel like running away.

Fear is a sneaky feeling that can pop up when we try something new or face something unknown. It's like our body's alarm system that helps us be careful and stay safe. For example, the fear of a hot stove keeps us from touching it and getting hurt.

Chapter 7: The Rainbow of Surprises

Imagine you're walking outside after a rainy day, and suddenly, a bright rainbow arches across the sky. That's a surprise! It's like opening a gift you didn't know about, or jumping up when a friend shouts "Boo!" Surprise is the feeling we get when something happens that we didn't expect at all. It can make our eyes go wide and our mouths drop open.

Sometimes surprises are exciting, like finding out you're going to your favorite park. Other times, they can be startling, like a loud noise that you didn't see coming. Surprises can make our hearts do a little skip and then dance to a faster beat.

Chapter 8: The Warmth of Love

Close your eyes and think about a loving hug, the comfort of snuggling with your pet, or the joy from a best friend's smile. That's love! It's a special kind of warmth that fills our hearts when we care for someone. Love can be compared to a cozy, gentle sunshine that nurtures a garden, helping all sorts of beautiful feelings bloom and grow.

Love is about sharing, whether it's your favorite toy, a helping hand to a friend in need, or saying sweet things to your family. It's a unique kind of happiness that not only makes you feel good but also brings a glow to those around you.

Chapter 9: The Whirlwind of Frustration

Frustration can feel like a whirlwind swirling inside, tossing your thoughts and feelings around. When you're frustrated, you might clench your fists, furrow your brow, or feel a storm of sighs coming out. It's like trying to solve a puzzle where the pieces don't quite fit, or reaching for a cookie jar that's just too high.

Frustration happens when things don't go as planned or when something feels too hard to do. Maybe it's a math problem that seems impossible, or perhaps it's when you're trying to build a tower of blocks, and it keeps tumbling down.

Frustration is that twisty, tangled feeling inside when you just can't seem to get what you want.

Chapter 10: The Mist of Disappointment

Disappointment can feel like a balloon losing air, slowly and sadly. When you're disappointed, your shoulders might droop like heavy branches, and your smile might turn into a frown. Disappointment is that sinking feeling when something you were excited about doesn't happen or isn't as good as you expected. It's like expecting a sunny day, but instead, it rains.

Disappointment is a natural feeling, like a cloudy sky in our hearts. It happens when things don't go the way we hoped, like if a playdate gets canceled, or you don't get the part you wanted in the school play. It's normal to feel this way, but what matters is how we find our way through the cloudy mist.

Chapter 11: The Breezy Day of Excitement

Excitement is like a sunny day with a playful breeze! When you're excited, it's like the wind is tickling you, making your eyes twinkle and your words zoom out fast like leaves dancing in the wind. This feeling is as fun as watching leaves swirl around on a windy day, full of bright colors and happy energy.

Think of the times when you can't wait for something wonderful to happen, like a birthday party, a trip to the zoo, or opening a brand-new book. Excitement is that bubbly, giggly feeling in your tummy, just like when you run and play outside on a breezy day, feeling happy and free.

Chapter 12: The Cloudy Day of Disgust

Disgust is like scrunching your nose when you smell something bad or looking away from something yucky. It's that "Ew!" feeling when you see, smell, or taste something you don't like, such as spoiled food or a messy, muddy puddle.

Think of disgust as your body's way of being a superhero. It tells you, "This might not be good!" like a superhero warning you about a muddy puddle that could ruin your clean shoes. It's completely okay to feel this way, but it's good to know why some things make us feel "Ew!"

Chapter 13: When Emotions Mix — Confusing Clouds

Have you ever felt like a smoothie made of different fruits, each taste swirling together to make something new? Sometimes, we can feel happy because we played with our friends, but also a bit sad because it's time to say goodbye. Or maybe we're excited about a family trip but nervous about the long ride. This is called having mixed emotions, and it's perfectly normal!

Think of your heart as the sky. Usually, the sky is clear with one kind of weather, like sunny or rainy. But sometimes, the sky gets creative and mixes them, creating a rainbow or a warm sunshower. Our emotions can do the same thing — mix together to make new, interesting feelings.

Chapter 14: Understanding Others – Empathy Breezes

Imagine you have a superpower that allows you to feel what someone else is feeling just by looking at them. That warm wind that helps you feel the same breeze as others is called empathy. Empathy is when we understand and share the feelings of our friends and family. It's like when you see a friend fall down and feel sorry for them because you know it hurts.

Empathy is like the gentle breeze that connects us all. It whispers to us how others might be feeling. When we listen to that breeze, we can be a good friend, a caring sibling, or a helpful classmate.

Chapter 15: Navigating Hard Feelings – The Compass of Control

Sometimes, we might feel a bit like we're lost at sea when we experience tough feelings like jealousy and envy. Imagine jealousy as a green wave that rises when someone has something that we wish for ourselves. Envy is similar, but it's more like a whispering wind, telling us that we want to be like someone else because they have what we think is cool or better.

These feelings are normal, but just like a ship uses a compass to find its way, we can learn to steer through these choppy waters. Remember, it's okay to feel this way, but it's not okay to act mean or hurt others because of our feelings.

Chapter 16: Weather Report – Checking In With Yourself

Just like the weather changes from sunny to rainy or windy, our feelings change too. It's important to know what kind of 'emotional weather' we have inside us each day. Are you feeling sunny and bright, or is there a storm brewing? Checking in with your feelings is like being your own weather forecaster.

Every morning, you can ask yourself, "How am I feeling today?" You might be happy, sad, excited, or maybe a mix of many feelings. Talking about these feelings with someone you trust can be like sharing the daily weather report – it helps others know what to expect and how to support you.

The Journey Continues

Hey there, amazing explorers! You've learned so much about the weather of your emotions, from sunny smiles to stormy frowns, and even rainbow surprises. But guess what? This is just the beginning of a fantastic journey! Your feelings are like a big, beautiful sky that changes a lot, and there's always more to discover.

Every day is a chance to learn more about your feelings. Are they wild like a windy day or calm like a quiet night? Remember, no matter what, your feelings are okay, and you're doing great at understanding them.

Keep talking about how you feel, and don't forget to listen to your friends' weather reports, too. Helping each other is what makes this journey extra special.

Glossary of Emotions and Feelings

Hello, young explorers! This part of the book is your guide to understanding the different feelings we've talked about. If you find a word that's as puzzling as a riddle, come here and you'll discover what it means!

- **Happiness:** It's like a warm, sunny day inside your heart.
- **Sadness:** Feeling blue, like when the sky is grey and you wish it would rain to match your mood.
- **Anger:** It's like a little fire inside that flares up when things don't go as you hoped.
- **Fear:** This feeling is the butterflies in your tummy when something scares you.
- **Surprise:** It's like finding a hidden treasure where you least expect it!
- **Love:** It feels like the biggest, warmest hug that makes you feel safe and happy.
- **Jealousy:** Wanting what someone else has, like eyeing a friend's ice cream and wishing it was yours.
- **Envy:** Similar to jealousy, it's when you really wish you had something that someone else has, like a shiny new bike.
- **Frustration:** It's like being a bird that's trying to fly against a strong wind, finding it hard to move forward.
- **Disappointment:** Feeling let down, like expecting a sunny day but getting rain instead.
- **Excitement:** It's the bubbly, fizzy feeling inside when you can't wait for something fun to happen.
- **Disgust:** It's like scrunching your nose at something stinky or yucky.

Each of these emotions is a unique color in the big rainbow of how we feel. Understanding them helps us navigate the wonderful world of our feelings!